One Stop Thematic Units

Swing into Spring!

Seasons in God's World

Deborah Saathoff and Jane Jarrell

Illustrator
Dan Farris

CPH
SAINT LOUIS

Contents

Introduction _____ **4**

**Blowing into Spring with
March Winds and Shamrocks** _____ **6**

April Showers _____ **30**

Mothers and May Flowers _____ **48**

Dear Teachers and Parents,

Swing Into Spring is a collection of ideas divided into three sections: *Blowing into Spring with March Winds and Shamrocks, April Showers,* and *Mothers and May Flowers.* Each section contains suggestions and directions for your classroom in the following areas:

Room Decor: Creating a visual environment gives children the opportunity to instantly see the theme for a particular unit. It also helps to stimulate positive thoughts of making learning fun as soon as they walk into the room. An inspiring room decor opens their imagination to all the possibilities available as they begin to learn.

Story Time and Reading Center: *Blessed is he who keeps the words of prophecy in this book* (Revelation 22:7). Opening a child's mind to reading lays a foundation for learning that is unmatched. Opening a child's mind to the Bible builds a foundation for eternity. A suggested list of books to match the theme is listed in this section to share with the children and to leave available for their own exploration. (Please note that some of the books are noted as out of print, but may still be available through the Internet, at libraries, or in personal collections.)

Language and Alphabet Skills: A thematic approach to language and the alphabet gives the child a great way to remember the basics. Each section offers suggestions for activities, games, and ideas for stretching these basic skills.

Places to Go and People to See: This section helps make it all real by offering a "real life" approach to the lessons being shared. You will find many suggestions for field trips and guest speakers related to the theme.

Music! Music! Music!: *Speak to one another with psalms, hymns and spiritual songs. Sing and make music in your heart to the Lord* (Ephesians 5:19). Music makes a heart joyful. Music also enriches the learning opportunities for children. Learning thematic songs adds another dimension to each lesson.

Movement: Movement offers active ways to experience the lesson being shared through exercise and games. It also gives everyone an opportunity to stretch, wiggle, and laugh. Movement encourages fun and thematic ideas for a break in the day.

Imaginative Play: Props and playthings that further enhance and encourage playing are suggested in this section. This offers the children an opportunity to really pretend to "be" and experience part of the theme.

Home Living Center: Here you will find suggestions for thematic additions to your year-round home living center.

Blocks Center: You will find suggestions for items to add and activities to encourage that build on the theme.

Sensory Table: The table you fill with sand, water, or other materials to encourage and build the exploration of the sense of touch can also be tailored to build on the theme. Included in this section are suggestions for ways to do that.

Science: Some simple science experiments and explorations related to the theme are found in this section.

Math: Number recognition, one-to-one correspondence, counting, patterns, and shapes make up a preschooler's math curriculum. You will find thematic suggestions for these kinds of activities in this section.

Arts and Crafts: Included here are instructions for items to make that relate to the theme.

Snack Time: This section offers recipes and suggestions for treats that build on the theme. (Please note that the ingredient lists only tell you the items needed. Please adjust amounts according to your class size.)

Faith Foundations: One way to make God's love appear real to a preschooler is through discussions about tangible things. This section offers suggestions for applying Scripture to the lesson and include activities and questions to help further the discussion.

Ultimately, Faith Foundations becomes the center for all of the other ideas in hopes of helping to lead little ones to Christ. By no means is this considered the only place to build the faith of the little ones in your care. Simply pointing out to two friends working cooperatively in the blocks center, "I like the way you are working so nicely together. Isn't it wonderful that God gives us friends?" is just one way to integrate the reality of God and His love for us into every activity.

Use these ideas as printed, adapt them, pick and choose, or modify them to fit your needs. We hope this will be both a resource and a springboard of ideas that will be a blessing to you and your children.

Deb and Jane

March

Blowing into Spring with March Winds and Shamrocks

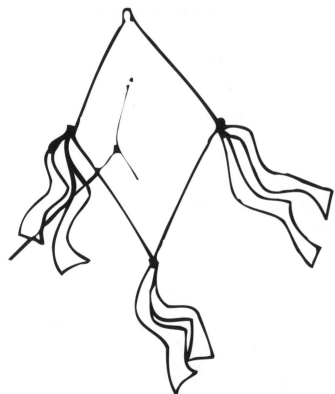

Room Decor

✔ Hang kites from the ceiling.

✔ Attatch ribbons to fans.

✔ Hang windsocks from the ceiling.

✔ Hang cotton ball clouds from the ceiling.

✔ Hang shamrocks and pots of gold from the ceiling.

✔ Display a large kite on the classroom door.

✔ Place a cloud blowing in the wind on the classroom door.

✔ Hang pinwheels from the ceiling.

✔ Make a large pinwheel for the classroom door.

✔ Hang windmills from the ceiling.

✔ Display a large windmill on the classroom door.

✔ Make your own bulletin board border using kites, windmills, or clouds blowing wind. (Make your own patterns or use patterns on pages 10 and 11.)

Story Time and Reading Center

Wind

Dorros, Arthur. *Feel the Wind*

Hutchins, Pat. *The Wind Blew*

Lasky, Kathryn. *The Gates of the Wind*

Mitra, Annie. *Chloe's Windy Day*

*MacDonald, Elizabeth. *The Very Windy Day*

*McKay, Louise and George. *Marny's Ride with the Wind*

Orser, Stanton. *Dancing with the Wind*

Pratt, Pierre. *Follow That Hat*

Purdy, Carol. *Iva Dunnit and the Big Wind*

Slater, Teddy and Bill Langley. *Walt Disney's Winnie the Pooh and the Blustery Day*

*This book is out of print, but may still be available through the Internet, at libraries, or in personal collections.

General Spring

Allington, Richard and Kathleen Krull. *Spring*

Ehlert, Lois. *Feathers for Lunch*

McLerran, Alice. *The Mountain That Loved a Bird*

Rockwell, Anne. *My Spring Robin*

Zion, Gene. *Really Spring*

St. Patrick's Day Books

Bunting, Eve. *St. Patrick's Day in the Morning*

Gibbons, Gail. *St. Patrick's Day*

Bible Story Books

Cook, Jean Thor. *Jesus Calms the Storm* (CPH, Arch Book)

Courtney, Claudia. *Blow* (CPH, Phonetic Bible Stories)

Places to Go and People to See

✗ Find open places to fly kites.

✗ Visit an airport or airfield to see windsocks in use.

✗ Visit a weather station.

✗ Visit a windmill.

✗ Attend a St. Patrick's Day parade.

✗ Invite a meteorologist to come and talk to your class about wind and rain. (Preview April!)

✗ Invite someone who pilots a craft affected by winds (such as a glider pilot, sailboat captain, hot-air balloon pilot) to talk to your class.

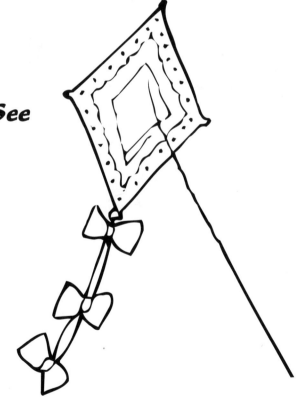

Language and Alphabet Skills

✔ Use the windmill pattern provided on this page for each letter of the alphabet you are emphasizing. Write the uppercase letter in the base of the windmill. Laminate. Cut out small circles that will fit on the windmill blades. On each circle write a lowercase alphabet letter. Laminate. Attach small pieces of Velcro to the back of the letters and to the front of each windmill blade so the children can match the lowercase letters to the uppercase letters.

✔ Make a simple windsock and label it with the letter you are emphasizing. Keep a collection of magazines, catalogs, and scissors near the windsock. Have the children cut out pictures of items that begin with the chosen letter and place them in the windsock. At the end of the day or during language time, "blow" the ideas across a bulletin board or simply take them out, one by one, and name them.

✔ Find pictures in magazines, newspapers, catalogs, or advertisements that show people or objects in the wind. Cut out the pictures and paste them on brightly colored pieces of construction paper and laminate. Let the children make up stories about what is happening in each picture.

St. Patrick's Day

✔ Spray paint juice can lids gold to look like gold coins. Cover two or more coffee cans or large butter tubs with black construction or contact paper to look like pots. Label the pots with letters you are studying. Cut out small pictures or use small stickers of objects that begin with the chosen letter. Children can match the picture to the correct letter.

✔ Cover a comfortable chair with a green sheet or a large tablecloth decorated with shamrocks, and place it in the reading center.

Music! Music! Music!

✔ "Spring" from Vivaldi's "The Four Seasons"
✔ "Let's Go Fly a Kite" from Walt Disney's "Mary Poppins"
✔ "It's a Very Blustery Day Today" from Walt Disney's
   "The Many Adventures of Winnie the Pooh"
✔ Irish dance tunes

Modify some old familiar tunes with a wind theme.

This is the Way the Wind Does Blow

Melody: *"Here We Go Round the Mulberry Bush"*
   This is the way the wind does blow,
   The wind does blow, the wind does blow.
   This is the way the wind does blow,
   Through branches of the trees.
   (Everybody blow!)

Blow, Blow, Blows the Wind

Melody: *"Row, Row, Row Your Boat"*
   Blow, blow, blows the wind
   Gently through my hair.
   Merrily, merrily, merrily, merrily,
   Blows the sweet, fresh air.

Mary Had a Little Kite

Melody: *"Mary Had a Little Lamb"*
   Mary had a little kite, little kite,
      little kite.
   Mary had a little kite,
   It flew high in the sky.

Movement

- ✔ Walk *against* a strong wind, then walk as if walking *with* a strong wind.
- ✔ Pretend your arms are flags flying in the breeze: a gentle breeze, a strong wind, a gale, then slow back down again.
- ✔ Fly like a kite.
- ✔ Swing on swings and feel the wind.
- ✔ Play with fireplace bellows.
- ✔ Dance an Irish Jig.

Directions for a simple Irish Jig:

1. Put your weight on your left foot and lift your right foot off the ground. Hop on your left foot once.
2. Hop on your left foot again, bringing your right foot back behind your left foot.
3. Shift your weight onto your right foot, leaving your left foot in the air. (*Use the phrase "hop, hop back" for the above three movements.*)
4. Then hop on your right foot.
5. Alternate feet, left-right-left-right. (*Use the phrase "hop, hop back, hop 1-2-3-4."*)

* You can alternate to the other side by reversing the left and right directions.

Imaginative Play

- ✗ Streamers to run and play with
- ✗ Fireplace bellows
- ✗ Pinwheels
- ✗ Paper fans (commercial and handmade)
- ✗ Scarves
- ✗ Bubbles
- ✗ Balloons

St. Patrick's Day

- ✗ Leprechaun hats (green derby hats)
- ✗ Shillelaghs
- ✗ Pots of gold

Sensory Table

Wind

- ✗ Fill with bubble solution and provide lots of bubble wands for blowing bubbles.
- ✗ Fill with feathers. (Available at craft stores.)

St. Patrick's Day

- ✗ Fill with clover leaves
- ✗ Fill with rice that has been dyed green.
- ✗ Spray paint large dry beans with gold spray paint. Hide the gold beans in the green rice for children to find.

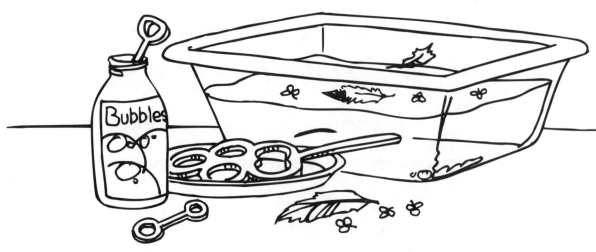

Home Living Center

✘ Fans
✘ Weather vane
✘ Wind chimes

Blocks Center

Wind
✘ Add paper fans to blow towers down.

St. Patrick's Day
✘ Add shamrock stickers to place on blocks.
✘ Include gold coins to hide in block structures.

Science

✔ Make a windsock (directions are included under "Arts and Crafts") or a wind vane (directions on page 16) and determine the direction of the wind.

✔ Or if you prefer an even lower-tech method: go outside on a mildly windy day. Allow the children to collect a few fallen petals, leaves, or pluck a few blades of grass and toss the items into the air. (Make sure the children have plenty of room between them before they throw!) Watch which way the wind blows the items.

✔ Study how animals and plants use the wind. Spiders use it for ballooning. Animals use it to hunt and to avoid being hunted. Plants use it to send seeds for dandelions, maple trees, and mushroom spores.

✔ Learn to identify the types of clouds.
Go outside and identify the clouds each day.
Chart the different kinds of clouds you find.

Cumulus clouds are puffy,
white clouds seen in fair weather.

Cumulonimbus clouds are tall,
dark, puffy clouds that mean rain
or snow is coming.

Cirrus clouds are high,
feathery, wispy clouds
(also indicating bad weather).

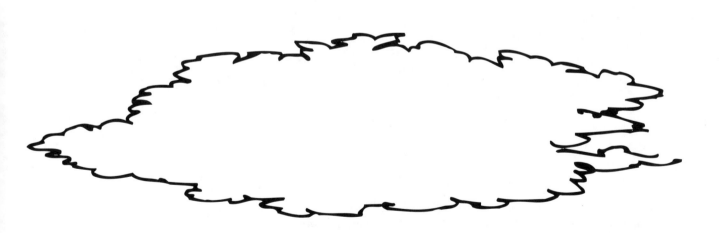

Stratus clouds are a layer or sheet
of dull gray clouds, usually with drizzle.

Weather Vane

You Will Need:

1 straw per vane

2 triangles cut from thin cardboard per vane

1 straight pin per vane

1 pencil per vane

1 yogurt container per vane

Modeling clay or play dough

Glue

Nail

How to Do:

1. Use the nail to poke a small hole in the bottom of the yogurt container. (Do this ahead of time.)
2. Cut a slit in each end of the straw. (Do this ahead of time.)
3. Insert one triangle in each slit so that it looks like an arrow. (See diagram.)
4. Glue the triangles in place.
5. Stick the straight pin through the middle of the straw and into the pencil's eraser. (Make sure the straw can swing freely.)
6. Turn the yogurt container upside down so that the bottom is now the top.
7. Anchor the container to the surface using clay or play dough.
8. Insert the pencil into the hole in the yogurt container.
9. Watch to see which way the wind blows!

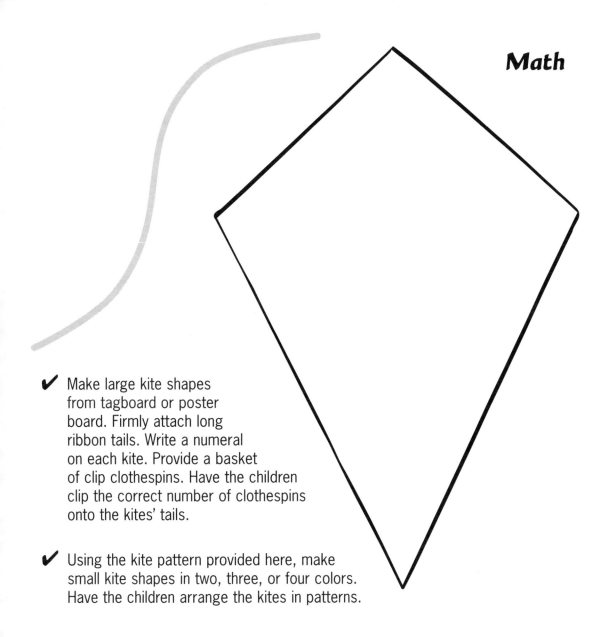

✔ Make large kite shapes from tagboard or poster board. Firmly attach long ribbon tails. Write a numeral on each kite. Provide a basket of clip clothespins. Have the children clip the correct number of clothespins onto the kites' tails.

✔ Using the kite pattern provided here, make small kite shapes in two, three, or four colors. Have the children arrange the kites in patterns.

✔ Make (or use) a simple game spinner (directions following). Let the children blow on the spinner. When it stops, have them count out that number of cotton balls (clouds) or kite shapes.

Simple Spinner

How to Do:
1. Draw a circle on a piece of paper.
2. Divide it into the desired number of sections.
3. Write a numeral in each section.
4. Glue the paper onto a piece of Styrofoam or heavy cardboard.
5. Make an arrow from thin cardboard shorter than the diameter of your circle.
6. Put a push pin through the center of the arrow, then push it through the center of the circle. (Make sure the arrow swings very freely.)

✔ Adapt the windmill pattern below to make various sets of windmill bases and blades (keep the base and blades separate). Vary the number of blades for each set, matching numerals that have been written on each windmill base. Laminate all pieces. Attach small pieces of Velcro to the back of the blades and to the front of each windmill so the children can match the correct set of blades to each windmill base.

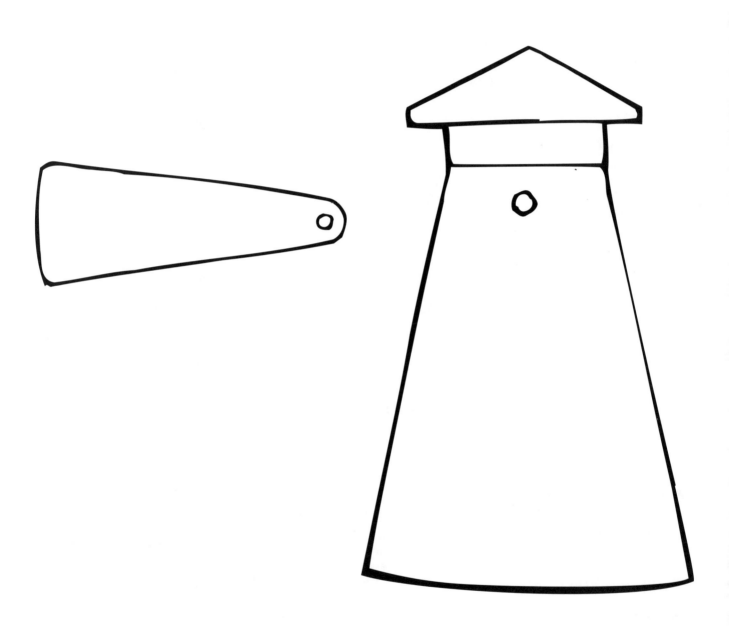

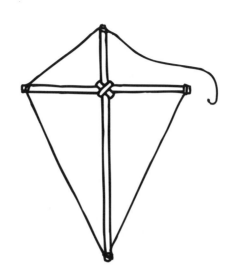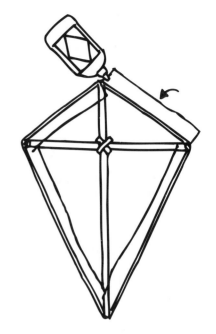

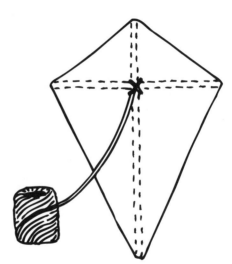

Let's Go Fly a Kite

You Will Need:

2 sticks (one longer than the other)

Tape

Ball of string

Scissors

Tissue paper

Glue, optional

Crepe paper streamers or a cloth
cut into long streamers

How to Do:

1. Make a cross with the two sticks. (The long stick up/down and the shorter stick across.) Secure by wrapping the tape around the center of the two sticks.
2. Tie the string to the end of one stick. Attach the string to the end of the next stick and continue until it forms the outline of a kite. Secure the string to the first end and cut. (See diagram.)
3. Fold the tissue paper over the front frame of the kite by folding the edges over the string. Secure the tissue paper with tape or glue.
4. Attach a crepe paper or cloth streamer to the end of the tissue paper kite by tying it onto the longer stick.
5. Tie the loose end of a ball of string to the center of the kite where the two sticks cross. Hold the ball of string and release the kite into the wind.

Super-Simple Bag Kites

You Will Need:

1 plastic shopping bag with handles per kite
1 ball of string per kite
3 lengths of ribbon per kite (2´ each)
Stapler

How to Do:

1. Tie the shopping bag handles together with the end of the ball of string.
2. Staple the lengths of ribbon to the bottom of the bag to make kite tails.
3. Go outside and start running.
4. When the bag fills with air, slowly let out the string and watch the kite soar and dive.

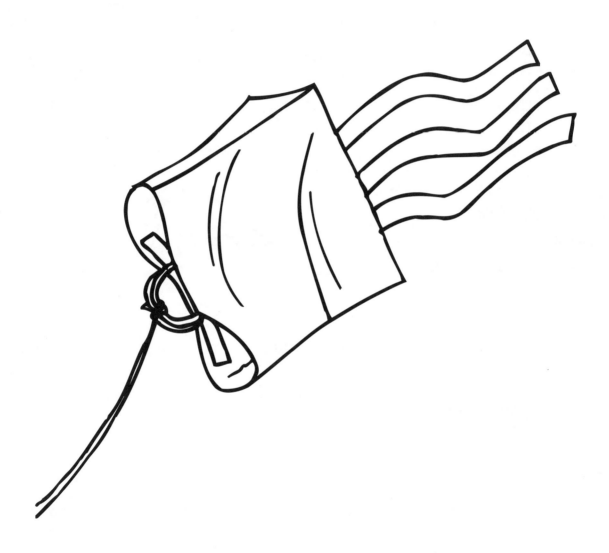

Twirling Pinwheel

You Will Need:

Square sheet of paper
Crayons or markers
Ruler
Scissors
Straight pin
Pencil with an eraser

How to Do:

1. Decorate the paper square with crayons or markers.
2. Draw diagonal lines, corner to corner (see diagram).
3. Draw a circle, about the size of a penny, in the center of the paper where the lines cross.
4. Cut the paper on the lines but do **not** cut inside the circle.
5. Bend the bottom-left corner of each section (A, B, C, D on diagram) into the center of the circle. Put a straight pin through all four corners. Then push the pin through the center of the paper where the lines cross.
6. Stick the pin into the eraser of the pencil.

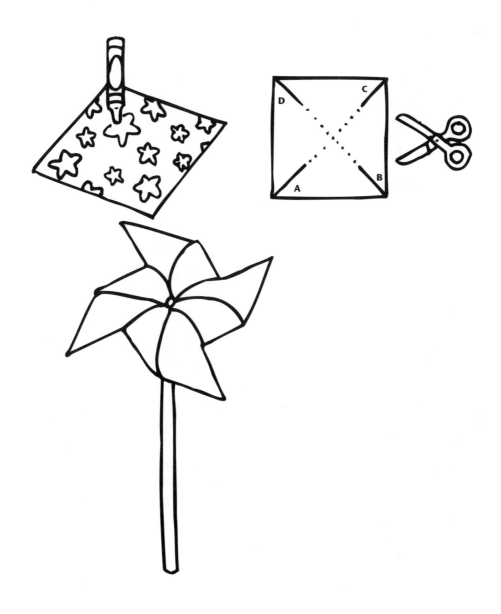

21

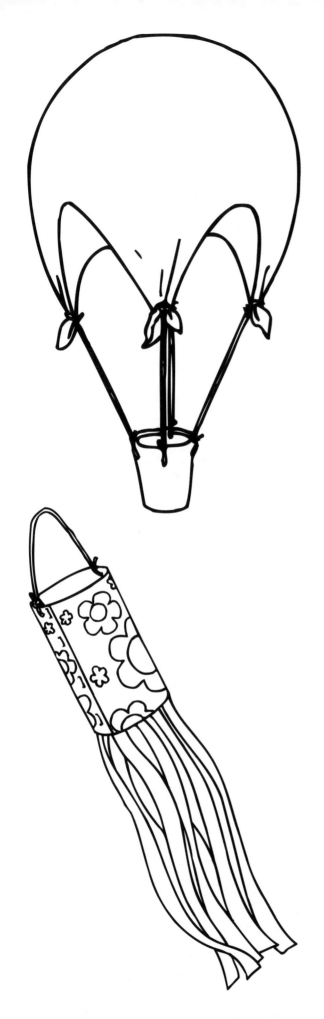

Parachute Flying in the Air

You Will Need:
Handkerchief
String
Small Dixie cup
Hole punch

How to Do:
1. Tie a piece of string to each corner of the handkerchief.
2. Punch four holes around the top of a Dixie cup. The holes should be on four opposite sides.
3. Tie the strings to the four holes of the Dixie cup.
4. Stand on something high and drop the parachute. Air will fill the handkerchief and make the parachute float.
 * For faster flying, place little pebbles in the Dixie cup to give the bottom extra weight.

Whimsical Windsock

You Will Need:
Construction paper
Stickers or stamps and ink pads
Tape and/or stapler
Hole punch
8″ pieces of yarn
Crepe paper

How to Do:
1. Decorate one side of a 9″ x 12″ sheet of construction paper with stickers or stamps.
2. Tape or staple the decorated paper together into a cylinder.
3. Using a hole punch, punch two holes on either side of the top of the paper cylinder.
4. Thread the yarn through each hole and tie into a knot.
5. Cut different colors of crepe paper into 12″ streamers.
6. Tape or staple the streamers onto the bottom of the windsock.

22

Accordion Fans

You Will Need:

Colored paper (6″ x 18″ is a good size)
Stamps and washable ink pad
Paper clip

How to Do:

1. Decorate the piece of paper with favorite stamps and ink.
2. Take one sheet of colored paper and fold 1″ down. Turn the paper over and fold 1″ down. Repeat this back and forth process until the entire piece of paper is folded into an accordion fan shape.
3. Fold the bottom up 1″ and secure with a paper clip.
4. Use the fans to feel the wind.

St. Patrick's Day Hat

You Will Need:

2 sheets of newspaper
Masking tape
Collage items
White craft glue

How to Do:

1. Center two single pages or one sheet of newspaper over the child's head.
2. Hold the paper down over the crown of the child's head. Wrap masking tape around and around to form the crown of the hat.
3. Roll the edges of the newspaper tightly toward the crown to form the brim of the hat. Secure with masking tape.
4. Decorate the hat with collage items such as green tissue paper, markers, crayons, feathers, glitter, buttons, and shamrocks.

Rice Shamrocks

You Will Need:

Rice

Green food coloring

Paper towels

Construction paper

Shamrock stencils

Pencils

Scissors

Paint brush

Glue

How to Do:

1. **Do this step at least one day ahead:**
   Place rice in a small amount of water to which green food coloring has been added. Let the rice soak until desired shade of green has been reached. Spread the rice out onto paper towels to dry.
2. Trace and cut out shamrock shapes.
3. Brush the shamrock shapes lightly with the glue. Sprinkle the green rice over the shamrock shape.

Pudding Paint

You Will Need:

Pistachio pudding,
  prepared according to package directions

Medium bowl, to prepare pudding

Spoons

Plastic cafeteria trays or aluminum cookie sheets

Green cherries, optional

How to Do:

1. Prepare pudding according to package directions.
2. Spoon the pudding onto the cafeteria trays or aluminum cookie sheets.
3. Let the children finger paint in the pudding to create their designs.
4. Decorate the works of art with green cherries.

* To save the fingerpainting, press a piece of paper onto the pudding design and carefully remove.

Snack Time

Kite Bites

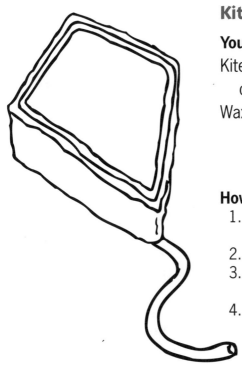

You Will Need:
Kite-shaped or diamond-shaped
   cookie cutters
Waxed paper

Ingredients:
Bread slices
Favorite sandwich meats
   (try corned beef)
String cheese or red licorice
   strings
Squirtable Cheese

How to Do:
1. Place the bread slices on the waxed paper and cut out the kite shapes with the cookie cutters.
2. Prepare favorite sandwiches using the kite-shaped breads.
3. Place a piece of string cheese or red licorice at the bottom of the kite sandwich for the kite string.
4. Decorate the top of the kite sandwich with the squirtable cheese.

Puffy White Meringue Clouds
(Sailing in the Wind)

You Will Need:
Rotary beaters
Large bowl
Large spoon
Measuring cup
Cookie sheet
Parchment paper
Oven

Ingredients:
6 egg whites
½ teaspoon cream of tartar
1 cup sugar

How to Do:
1. Preheat oven to 275°.
2. Cover a cookie sheet with parchment paper.
3. In a large bowl, beat the egg whites and cream of tartar until foamy.
4. Add sugar, one tablespoon at a time. Continue beating until the mixture is stiff.
5. Spoon meringue "clouds" onto the cookie sheet.
6. Place in the oven for 1 ½ hours. Turn the oven off and leave the meringues inside **with the door closed** for another hour.
* When working with the rotary beaters, talk about the air and wind.

Balloons Blowing in the Wind

You Will Need:

Platter

Knife

Ingredients:

Frozen, pre-prepared round waffles or pancakes

Small tub of strawberry cream cheese

Fresh strawberries, washed and chopped

Strips of bacon, cooked

How to Do:

1. Prepare the waffles/pancakes according to package directions.
2. Spread a waffle/pancake with strawberry cream cheese, sprinkle with strawberries, and top with second waffle/pancake.
3. Place the cooked bacon slices at the bottom of the waffle to form the balloon strings.

Tortilla Shamrocks

You Will Need:

Cutting board

Shamrock cookie cutter

Cookie sheet

Pastry brush

Measuring cups

2 small bowls

Oven

Ingredients:

12 large flour tortillas

½ cup butter, melted

½ cup sugar

Green food coloring

1 tablespoon cinnamon

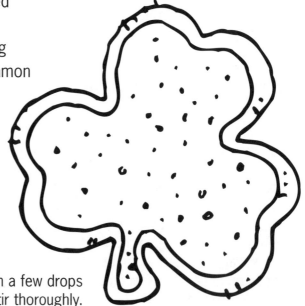

How to Do:

1. Preheat oven to 350°.
2. Place the tortillas on a cutting board and cut with the shamrock cookie cutter.
3. Place the cut tortillas on the cookie sheet.
4. Brush the tortilla shamrocks with melted butter. (Do this step quickly or the tortillas will harden.)
5. In the second bowl thoroughly mix the sugar with a few drops of green food coloring. Add the cinnamon and stir thoroughly.
6. Sprinkle the cinnamon/sugar mixture over the tortillas.
7. Place in the oven and bake for 8–10 minutes.

St. Patrick's Day Snake Biscuits

You Will Need:
Cookie sheet
Bowl
Spoon
Waxed paper
Shamrock cookie cutter
Oven

Ingredients:
Refrigerated breadstick dough
Butter
Green food coloring

How to Do:
1. Place slightly softened butter into the bowl.
   Add food coloring and mix to combine the color.
2. Place the green butter mixture on the waxed paper and flatten into
   a pancake shape. Cover the top with wax paper and refrigerate.
3. Open the breadstick can and separate the breadsticks.
4. Roll each breadstick into a long tube shape and place
   on the cookie sheet. Curve the breadstick to form
   a slithering snake shape.
5. Bake according to package directions.
6. Cut out a shamrock shape from
   the butter pancake. Serve with
   warm snake biscuits.

Faith Foundations

God controls the wind (Mark 4:41). We can't see the wind, but we know it is there because we can see the results. We can feel it. We can see the leaves blow. We can feel our hair move. We can see the waves of the ocean hit the sand on the beach.

Just like we can't see the wind, we can't see God. But we know He is with us. We know this because we believe what the Bible teaches. We can see the world that God made and everything in it. God sent His only Son Jesus to be our Savior from sin. He gave us the Bible so that we can learn more about His awesome greatness.

Even though we can't see God, we can know that He is there. We can talk to Him in prayer. We can see His love in a parent's eyes. We can feel His gentle care in a warm hug. We can share His love when we give to a friend.

To build a faith foundation in the children during this unit, discuss how we know that God is with us even when we cannot see Him.

Scripture

Jesus Calms the Storm

A furious squall came up, and the waves broke over the boat, so that it was nearly swamped. Jesus was in the stern, sleeping on a cushion. The disciples woke Him and said to Him, "Teacher, don't You care if we drown?" He got up, rebuked the wind and said to the waves, "Quiet! Be still!" Then the wind died down and it was completely calm. He said to His disciples, "Why are you so afraid? Do you still have no faith?"

They were terrified and asked each other, "Who is this? Even the wind and the waves obey Him!" (Mark 4:37–41)

Questions

Q How do you know God is with you even when you can't see Him?

Q How do you feel when you know you have done what Jesus would have done for a friend?

Q How can you explain to a friend about something that you cannot see?

Activities

Wind Watchers

✗ Go for a walk on a windy day. Watch the trees bend, the flowers bow, and the water lap onto the shore. Talk about how we know that God is with us when we feel the winds blow.

Sharing God's Love

✗ Show others God's love by creating a special goody bag for them. Take the colorful windsock and staple the bottom closed. Fill it with candy, crayons, stickers, or gum. Put a little card on it that says: "God loves you and so do I." Put a big ribbon around the windsock and deliver it to someone's doorstep. This is a way to show God's love in a simple, yet special, way.

April

April Showers

Room Decor

✔ Hang miniature party favor umbrellas from the ceiling along with construction-paper raindrops.

✔ Hang construction paper or tagboard lightning bolts from the ceiling.

✔ Display a large umbrella door decoration.

✔ Place a picture of a child dressed for rain (raincoat, galoshes, umbrella) on the classroom door.

✔ Place cutouts of raindrops all over the door.

✔ Hang rainbows from the ceiling.

✔ Place a large rainbow on the wall, or door, or arch it over the doorway.

✔ Bulletin board idea: raindrops with letters of the alphabet raining down.

✔ Make your own bulletin board border of raindrops and rainbows.

Story Time and Reading Center

General Books

- Asch, Frank. *Skyfire*
- Brown, Jennifer Maze. *Hooray! It's a Duck Day* (CPH)
- Carle, Eric and Patricia Gauch. *The Little Cloud*
- Ehlert, Lois. *Planting a Rainbow*
- Freeman, Don. *A Rainbow of My Own*
- Kuskin, Karla. *James and the Rain*
- Mayer, Mercer. *Just a Rainy Day*
- *Serfozo, Mary. *Rain Talk*
- Shaw, Charles G. *It Looked Like Spilt Milk*
- *Skofield, James. *All Wet! All Wet!*
- Spier, Peter. *Noah's Ark*
- Spier, Peter. *Peter Spier's Rain*

* This book is out of print, but may still be available through the Internet, at libraries, or in personal collections.

Bible Story Books

- Curren, Joan. *Noah's 2-by-2 Adventure* (CPH, Arch Book)
- Courtney, Claudia. *Saved by Faith* (CPH, Phonetic Bible Stories)
- Simon, Mary Manz. *Drip Drop* (CPH, Hear Me Read Series)

Places to Go and People to See

✗ Visit a weather station.

✗ Visit your city's water treatment plant or reservoir.

✗ Take a rain walk complete with puddle splashes.

✗ Invite a meteorologist to speak to your class.

Language and Alphabet Skills

✔ Using the cloud pattern, make clouds out of poster board or heavy construction paper. Label each with a capital letter. Use the raindrop pattern here and construction paper to make several raindrops. Place a lowercase letter on each raindrop. Have the children match the correct raindrops to the clouds.

You may vary this activity by using the umbrella pattern on this page instead of clouds for the uppercase letters. Let the lowercase letters rain down onto the umbrella with the matching uppercase letter.

✔ Label cloud shapes with uppercase letters. Cut out and laminate large raindrops but do not label them. Place them with a collection of magazines, catalogs, scissors, and tape. Let the children cut out items from the magazines that begin with each cloud's letter. Tape the pictures to the raindrops. Place with the correct cloud.

✔ Collect pictures from newspapers, magazines, advertisements, and catalogs that show people and places with rain and/or rainbows. Laminate them. Let the children make up stories about what they think has just happened, is happening, or will happen next.

Music! Music! Music!

"Rain, Rain Go Away"
"It's Raining, It's Pouring"
"Raindrops Keep Falling on My Head"
"If All the Raindrops (Were Lemon
     Drops and Gumdrops)"
"Somewhere over the Rainbow"
"The Rainbow Connection"
     (from "The Muppet Movie")
"It Ain't Gonna Rain No More"

Movement

✔ Act out the water cycle: The water on the ground evaporates up into the air. Join together to form a cloud. The cloud gets bigger and bigger. Raindrops fall down to the earth, lie in a puddle, and finally evaporate into the air.

✔ Demonstrate all the ways to splash in a puddle.

✔ Walk as though you're walking through ooey-gooey mud.

✔ Pretend you're an umbrella folded up in the stand. You're picked up. Unfolded. Opened out. Carried through the rain. Closed. Folded. Returned to the rack.

✔ Shake large pieces of heavy poster board to make thunder. (Or bang pots and pans, hit a tambourine, or clap hands.)

Sensory Table

✗ Fill with water.
✗ Provide watering cans, eye droppers, and turkey basters.
✗ Dye the water blue.

Home Living Center

✗ Rain gauge
✗ Barometer
✗ Umbrellas
✗ Galoshes
✗ Raincoats
✗ Rain hats

Blocks Center

✗ Build a bridge over a rain-swollen creek.

Imaginative Play

✗ Umbrellas
✗ Galoshes
✗ Raincoats
✗ Rain hats

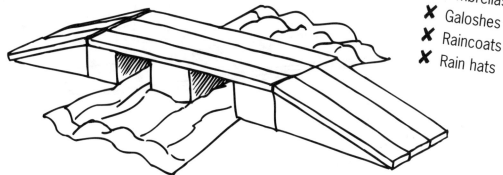

Science

How Plants Get a Drink of Rain

1. Purchase white carnations or use celery stalks with leaves.
2. Cut stems or stalks at an angle leaving about 3″ of stem.
3. Place water in clear containers filled with water.
4. Add a different color of food coloring to each container of water.
5. Flower petals and celery leaves will become the color of the water. (Flowers will begin to change within 2 hours. The celery may take overnight.)

Make a Rain Gauge

You Will Need:

Wide-mouthed plastic
   container with straight sides

Ruler

Permanent marker

How to Do:

1. Holding the ruler up to the container, use a permanent marker to mark each inch and fraction of an inch along the side.
2. Check the rain gauge each day for a month.
3. Chart the amount of rain per day (for a month).

Make It Rain!

1. Using a hot plate or stove, heat water in a kettle until it is boiling and producing a cloud of steam. (Make sure the children are carefully supervised and are observing from a safe distance.)
2. Hold a cold cookie sheet in the path of the steam. The vapor will quickly condense and little drops of water will form and fall.
3. Explain that real rain happens much more slowly. God makes the sun warm the water in rivers, lakes, and oceans. The water then evaporates, creating a rising vapor that cools and forms raindrops.

Make a Rainbow

On a sunny day (early morning or late afternoon are the best times because the sun's rays are the most slanted), stand in an open area with your back to the sun. Spray a fine mist of water in front of you. Look for the rainbow. (Try to find a dark background for the spray so the colors really stand out.) Rainbows form when raindrops are in the air while the sun is shining.

Math

Same or Different?

You Will Need:
2 clear glasses,
    one taller than the other
1 clear pitcher
Glass liquid measuring cup
Water

How to Do:
1. Pour equal amounts of water into each glass.
2. Ask the children which glass they think has the most water—the tall glass or the short glass.
3. Pour the water from one glass into the measuring cup. Mark the water line. Empty.
4. Pour the water from the second glass into the measuring cup.
5. Note that the level of the water is the same.
* You can use this activity as a springboard into a discussion about how some things may look different but can still be the same—like people. We all look different, but we are same in that God loves each one of us and sent Jesus to be our Savior.

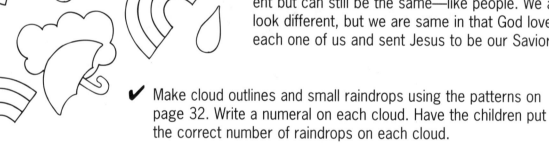

✔ Make cloud outlines and small raindrops using the patterns on page 32. Write a numeral on each cloud. Have the children put the correct number of raindrops on each cloud.

✔ Make several umbrellas using the umbrella pattern on page 32. On one set of umbrellas, write a numeral. Divide another set of umbrellas into various sections of color. Have the children match the umbrella with numerals to the umbrellas that have the same number of colored sections.

✔ Make umbrella patterns. Write a numeral on the handle of each umbrella. Have the children put the correct number of round stickers (like those used for garage sales) on each umbrella.

U is for Umbrella

You Will Need:

Various colors of construction paper
Scissors
String
Craft glue

How to Do:
1. Cut large circles from different colors of construction paper.
2. Cut the circles in half.
3. Glue one half-circle onto a large piece of paper. Glue three pieces of string reaching from the top center to the bottom of the half-circle, dividing the umbrella top into four equal sections. (See illustration.)
4. Cut out a 6″ piece of the brown construction paper about ½″ wide. Cut a little hook on the end to form the handle.
5. Glue the handle underneath the umbrella.
* Cut out raindrops to glue around the umbrella.

Rainy Day Dish Garden

Take a Walk and Gather:

Moss

Small weeds

Clover and greenery (Removed gently
   with their roots and some soil,
   and placed into a plastic bag.)

Small pebbles

Pieces of bark

Colored stones

Sticks

Purchase:

Little house

Little plastic animals

Pie plate or terra cotta plant dish

How to Do:
1. Put a layer of small pebbles in the bottom of the pie plate or terra cotta plant dish.
2. Cover the pebbles with soil.
3. Create large green areas with the moss.
4. Use your fingers to poke holes in the dirt and plant the small plants in them.
5. The small sticks can be used as borders for walkways made from pebble or grass seed.
6. Set the little house and plastic animals in the garden.

Rain Sticks

You Will Need:

Cardboard tube from wrapping paper or paper towels

Circles of heavy construction paper cut to be
    folded over the ends of the cardboard tube

White craft glue

Heavy colored tape, optional

Variety of dried beans, split peas, rice

Stickers or stamps and ink pads

Crayons or markers

How to Do:

1. Cover one end of the tube with a circle of construction paper by gluing the edges of the tube with craft glue or by taping with colorful heavy tape. Let glue dry before continuing.
2. Add a handful of a variety of dried beans, split peas, and/or rice to the tube.
3. Glue or tape another construction paper circle over the remaining open end of the tube. Let dry.
4. Decorate with markers, crayons, stickers, or stamps.
5. These can be used as rain sticks to mimic the sound of rain by turning **slowly** turning the tube back and forth, letting the beans/peas/rice slide from one end of the tube to the other.

Rain Prints

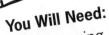

You Will Need:
White drawing paper or uncoated
  white paper plates
Powdered tempera paints or food coloring
Rain
White crayon, optional

How to Do:
1. Sprinkle different colors of powdered tempera paints or food coloring onto the construction paper or paper plate. (Protect your table with newspaper before adding food coloring because it could soak through the paper or plate.)
2. Set the paper/paper plate outside during a light rain. Carefully remove the paper from the rain and look at the colorful painted print.
   * For a batik effect, color the paper/plate with white crayon first before setting out in the rain.

Mud Mania Sculptures

You Will Need:
Mud
Pie and cupcake tins
Big spoons
Measuring cups
Small plastic buckets

How to Do:
Give the children a bucket of mud and ask them to create a mud sculpture (i.e. castles, towers, volcanoes, people).
* Try this inside with a plastic covering on the floor or outside after it rains. (Make sure the children's clothes are protected.)

Cereal Rainbows

You Will Need:
Brightly colored cereal
   (Froot Loops, Fruity Pebbles, etc.)
Waxed paper
White craft glue
Construction paper

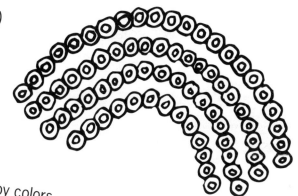

How to Do:
1. Place a sheet of waxed paper on the work surface. Pour the cereal out onto the waxed paper and sort it by colors.
2. Make a rainbow by gluing cereal pieces of the same color into semi-circle lines on the construction paper. Continue until all of the colors have been used. (See diagram.)

Rainbow Bubble Prints

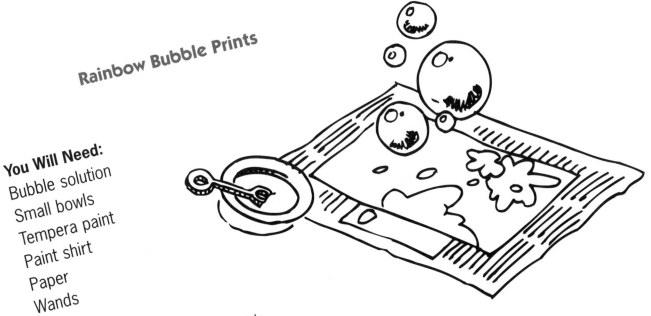

You Will Need:
Bubble solution
Small bowls
Tempera paint
Paint shirt
Paper
Wands

How to Do:
1. Pour a small amount of bubble solution into a bowl.
2. Add a few drops of tempera paint and stir. Make several different colors of bubble solution.
3. Let the children blow bubbles that pop on the paper, leaving splatters of color. Repeat using different colors until each child has a colorful splatter picture.

41

Snack Time

Silver Lining Cloud Cakes

You Will Need:

Waxed paper

Glass bowl for marshmallow creme

Ingredients:

1 store-bought angel food cake

1 jar marshmallow creme

Silver balls used for cake decorating

How to Do:

1. Place the waxed paper on a work surface.
2. Tear the angel food cake into small pieces.
3. Dip the angel food cake pieces into the marshmallow creme and then into the silver balls. Place on the wax paper.
* Serve the cloud cakes on a blue platter.

Puddle Punch

You Will Need:

Small watering can

Large cups

Plastic pitcher

Large spoon

Ingredients:

1 small can strawberry lemonade

1 liter bottle ginger ale

Crushed ice

How to Do:

1. Prepare the strawberry lemonade in the plastic pitcher according to the package directions.
2. Add crushed ice, stir to combine.
3. Pour the ginger ale into the small watering can. Then pour it into the large pitcher, resembling rain falling down. Stir to combine.
4. Pour the rain punch from the large pitcher into the small watering can for another shower into the large cups.
5. Add a colorful paper umbrella.

Silly Rain Soup

You Will Need:
Blender
Small bowls
Spoons

Ingredients:
1 bottle club soda
1 bottle pineapple juice
1 pint pineapple sherbet
Maraschino cherries for plopping into the soup like raindrops, optional

How to Do:
1. Add the first three ingredients to the blender. Blend to combine.
2. Pour into the small bowls. Plop the cherries in like raindrops.
* Use different colors of sherbet to form a rainbow in the rain soup.

Jell-O Raindrops

You Will Need:
9" x 13" glass dish
Measuring cups
Mashed potatoes
Pieces of cheese
Raindrop-shaped cookie cutter

Ingredients:
2 boxes blue Jell-O
Hot water
Cold water

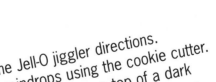

How to Do:
1. Prepare the Jell-O according to the Jell-O jiggler directions.
2. When the Jell-O has set, cut into raindrops using the cookie cutter.
3. To serve: Place a serving of mashed potatoes on top of a dark blue dinner plate. Cut out some lightning shapes from American cheese slices. Place the raindrops below the mashed potato cloud and in between the lightning cheese.

Ooey-Gooey Mud Pies

You Will Need:
Large, resealable plastic bag
Medium bowl
Measuring cups
Spoons
Small aluminum tins or muffin cups

Ingredients:
1 package Oreos
1 package chocolate pudding
Milk
Chocolate sprinkles
Gummi Worms, optional

How to Do:
1. Prepare the pudding according to package directions. Chill.
2. Place the Oreos in the resealable plastic bag and crush to coarsely chop the cookies. Add the crushed Oreos to the pudding as it chills.
3. Spoon the "mud" into the small aluminum tins and sprinkle with chocolate sprinkles. Add the Gummi Worms, if desired.

Rainbow Salad

You Will Need:
Large bowl
Spoon
Individual serving bowls or plates
Silverware

Ingredients:
Strawberries
Oranges
Pineapple
Green apples
Blueberries
Purple grapes
Mini-marshmallows

How to Do:
1. Follow the color order of the rainbow as you place the pieces of fruit into the salad bowl, one by one. Be sure to call attention to each fruit's color.
2. Stir to combine. Sprinkle in mini-marshmallow raindrops.

Rainbow Umbrella Cakes

You Will Need:
Umbrella-shaped cookie cutters
Waxed paper
6" skewers or lollipop sticks
Sugar shakers or a small sifter

Ingredients:
1 pre-prepared pound cake
Colored powdered sugars

How to Do:
1. Slice the pound cake into ½" slices. Place on waxed paper and cut into umbrella shapes.
2. Insert the lollipop sticks or the skewers into the bottom edge of the umbrella-shaped cake. (This will be the umbrella handle.)
3. Sprinkle the umbrellas with a rainbow of colored sugars.
* To serve: Place the umbrella cakes on a large platter and use a sprinkling of lemon drops for the rain.

Rainbow Confetti

You Will Need:
Several colorful paper sacks
Measuring cup
Large bowl
Colored ribbon

Ingredients:
2 cups Fruity Pebbles
1 cup Froot Loops
1 cup Gummi Bears (assorted colors)
1 cup Skittles
1 cup gumdrops
1 cup M&Ms
1 cup jelly beans

How to Do:
1. Place all of the ingredients into a large bowl and stir to combine.
2. Use the measuring cup to scoop the rainbow confetti into the colored paper sacks.

Rainbow Toast

You Will Need:

3 cups
Measuring cup
Small spoons
Waxed paper
Cookie sheet
Clean paint brushes
Oven

Ingredients:

1 cup milk
3 colors of food coloring
Slices of bread

How to Do:

1. Pour ⅓ cup of milk into each cup. Add drops of one food coloring to each cup and stir.
2. Place the bread slices on the waxed paper. Use the paint brushes and the three colors of milk to paint a rainbow on each slice of bread.
3. Place the painted bread slices on the cookie sheet and toast in an oven until golden brown.

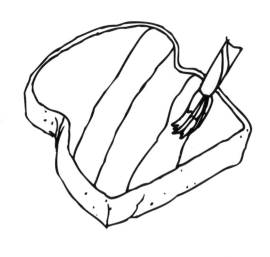

Faith Foundations

Have you ever seen the beautiful colors of a rainbow after a spring shower? Rainbows can appear in the sky if the sun shines while rain is in the air. The rainbow is more than just an arch of colors in the sky that is pretty to look at. It is a sign of God's promise to Noah never to flood the whole earth again (Genesis 9:13). When we see a rainbow, we can remember God's promise. God always keeps His promises (Hebrews 6:18).

To build a faith foundation in the children during this unit, take a look at what God tells us about the way we understand His promises.

Scripture

I have set My rainbow in the clouds, and it will be the sign of the covenant between Me and the earth (Genesis 9:13).

God did this so that, by two unchangeable things in which it is impossible for God to lie, we who have fled to take hold of the hope offered to us may be greatly encouraged. We have this hope as an anchor for the soul, firm and secure (Hebrews 6:18–19a).

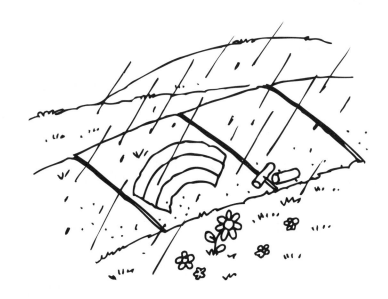

Questions

Q Why did God send a rainbow?

Q What other promises does God give us in the Bible?

Q How can we know that God always keeps His promises?

Activities

✘ Rainbows frequently appear in children's pictures. This is an opportunity for them to learn the proper order of colors in God's rainbow. Create a chart using the colors and number them 1 to 6. One being the top of the arch and 6 being the bottom. The order of the colors from 1 to 6 is: red, orange, yellow, green, blue, and purple. The red rays are always the longest rays in the rainbow and the purple rays are always the shortest.

✘ Draw a rainbow on the sidewalk using colored sidewalk chalks.

May

Mothers and May Flowers

Room Decor

✔ Hang flowers from the ceiling.

✔ Place flowers along the baseboards as if growing from the floor.

✔ Set pots of flowers around the room.

✔ Display a large flowerpot filled with flowers (each with a child's name) on the door as a door decoration.

✔ Use a floral air freshener.

✔ Bulletin Board: "Alphabet Blooms" with 26 flowers, each with a letter of the alphabet on its petals.

✔ Make your own bulletin board border of flowers.

Story Time and Reading Center

Flowers

- Bunting, Eve. *Flower Garden*
- Carle, Eric. *The Very Hungry Caterpillar*
- Ehlert, Lois. *Growing Vegetable Soup*
- Higgs, Liz Curtis. *The Parable of the Sunflower*
- Lionni, Leo. *The Alphabet Tree*
- Lobel, Anita. *Alison's Zinnia*
- Merrill, Claire. *A Seed Is a Promise*
- Florian, Douglas. *Vegetable Garden*
- Perkins, Lynne Rae. *Home Lovely*
- Stoker, Joann and Gerald. *ABC Book of Flowers for Young Gardeners*
- Turner, Ann. *Red Flower Goes West*
- Wolkstein, Diane. *Step by Step*

Mothers

- Bailey, Debbie. *My Mom*
- Butterworth, Nick. *My Mom Is Excellent*
- Eastman, Philip D. *Are You My Mother?*
- Hendry, Diana. *Back Soon*
- Huss, Sally. *I Love You with All My Hearts*
- Joosse, Barbara. *I Love You the Purplest*
- Mayer, Mercer. *Just for You*
- Munsch, Robert N. *Love You Forever*
- Porter-Gaylord, Laura. *I Love My Mommy Because*
- Ross, Katharine. *Mama Loves*
- Simmons, Jane. *Come Along, Daisy*
- Waddell, Martin. *Owl Babies*
- Wolfgram, Barbara. *I Know My Mommy Loves Me* (CPH)
- Zolotow, Charlotte. *This Quiet Lady*

People to See and Places to Go

✗ Visit an arboretum or botanical garden.

✗ Visit a farmer's market.

✗ Visit a farm.

✗ Visit a nursery.

✗ Take a nature walk and look at the spring plants growing.

✗ Visit a florist.

✗ Invite a nursery worker to speak to your class about growing plants.

✗ Visit or invite a farmer to speak to your class about planting and growing crops.

Language and Alphabet Skills

✔ Copy several flowerpot patterns. On each one write an uppercase letter. Make several flowers with lowercase letters printed on them. Have the children put the correct flowers into the pots.

✔ Vary the above by putting small pictures or stickers of items that begin with the desired letter on the flowers. Place the flowers into the pot that shows what letter begins with the sound in each flower's picture.

✔ Make 26 circular flower centers and several "daisy-like" petals using the patterns above. Write uppercase letters on the centers. Write lowercase letters on the petals. Let the children make flowers by matching centers with the correct petals.

✔ Cut out several pictures of mothers with children. Mount them on colorful construction paper and laminate. Let the children make up stories about the people, about what is happening, or about what just happened.

50

Music! Music! Music!

Planting

"The Farmer in the Dell"
"Let the Sunshine In"
"Heavenly Sunshine"
"Jesus Wants Me for a Sunbeam"
"Oats, Peas, Beans, and Barley Grow"
"Tiptoe through the Tulips"

Modify some familiar tunes with planting themes.

"The Farmer Plants the Seeds"

Melody: *"The Farmer in the Dell"*
> The farmer plants the seeds,
> The farmer plants the seeds,
> Heigh ho, the dairy oh,
> The farmer plants the seeds.

The seeds begin to sprout …
The plants begin to grow …
The farmer picks his crop …
Then we eat our food …

"I'm a Little Flower"

Melody: *"I'm a Little Teapot"*
> I'm a little flower,
> Watch me grow.
> I start from a seed
> But before you know
> I have pretty petals
> And a fragrance sweet
> Take a sniff,
> It's such a treat!

Mother's Day

"Shortnin' Bread"
"M-O-T-H-E-R"

Modify some familiar tunes with a Mother theme.

"I Love Mommy"

Melody: *"Are You Sleeping?"*
> I love Mommy,
> I love Mommy,
> Yes, I do!
> Yes, I do!
> Mommies are for hugging.
> Mommies are for kissing.
> I love you.
> I love you.

Movement
✓ Act like a seed sending out a tiny shoot. Slowly growing into a tall plant. Reaching for the sun.
✓ Gather a bouquet of flowers.

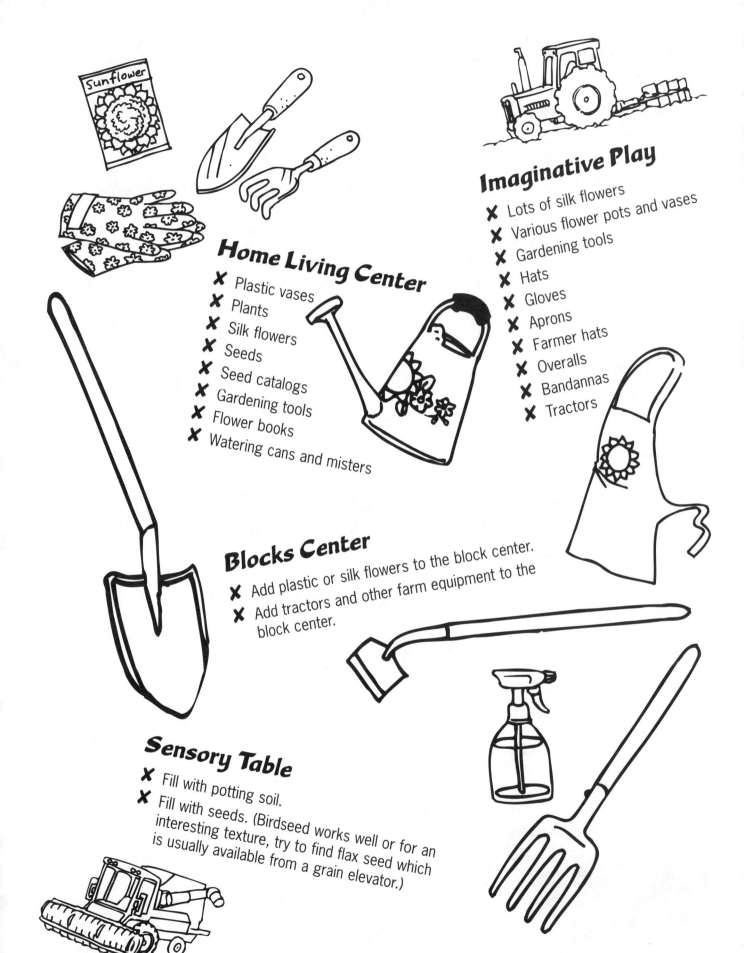

Imaginative Play

- ✗ Lots of silk flowers
- ✗ Various flower pots and vases
- ✗ Gardening tools
- ✗ Hats
- ✗ Gloves
- ✗ Aprons
- ✗ Farmer hats
- ✗ Overalls
- ✗ Bandannas
- ✗ Tractors

Home Living Center

- ✗ Plastic vases
- ✗ Plants
- ✗ Silk flowers
- ✗ Seeds
- ✗ Seed catalogs
- ✗ Gardening tools
- ✗ Flower books
- ✗ Watering cans and misters

Blocks Center

- ✗ Add plastic or silk flowers to the block center.
- ✗ Add tractors and other farm equipment to the block center.

Sensory Table

- ✗ Fill with potting soil.
- ✗ Fill with seeds. (Birdseed works well or for an interesting texture, try to find flax seed which is usually available from a grain elevator.)

52

Planting Seeds

✔ Plant bean seeds in a clear plastic cup. (Soak the beans overnight before planting.) Make sure to place the beans against the side of the cup to watch the roots go down and the shoots grow up.

✔ If you prefer, you can start the beans by letting the seed sprout without soil. Moisten a paper towel and place it in a small reclosable plastic bag. Place one or two bean seeds on the paper towel in the plastic bag. Tape the bag to the window or leave on a sunny windowsill. Squirt water into the bag each day and watch the seeds sprout. After about two weeks, the plants will need to be placed in soil.

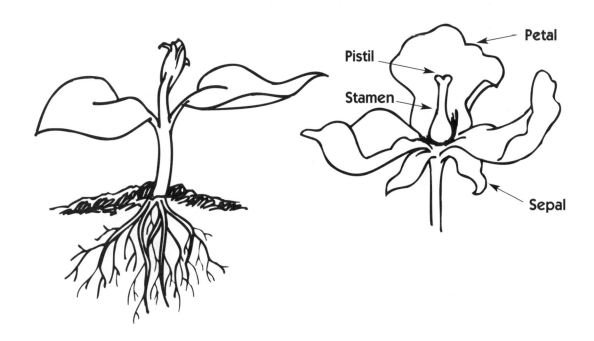

Plant Parts

✔ Learn the parts of a plant as the seeds sprout and grow: roots, stem, leaves, buds, flowers, and fruit.

✔ Get really adventurous and learn the flower parts. Bring in several flowers and learn to identify the parts of the flower. Use a magnifying glass while examining the parts.

Petal: attract insects

Sepal: the green petals that enclose and protect the bud

Pistil: (female part): includes the sticky top part that traps pollen from other plants (stigma), the stalk that holds the stigma (style), and the ovary which holds eggs that will become seeds when fertilized with pollen

Stamen: (male part): includes anther which produces pollen and the filament that holds up the anther

Some plants have separate male and female flowers.

Fruit or Vegetable?

✗ Sort real or plastic fruits and
vegetables by type, color, size, etc.

How Many Flowers Can You Name?

✔ Feature a Flower of the Day using flowers common to your area.

✔ Take a walk after studying several flowers and see how many you can identify.

Math

✔ Label envelopes or small plastic reclosable bags with numbers. Let the children count out the correct number of seeds into each envelope. (Large seeds like bean, pumpkin, or squash work best.)

✔ Using the patterns on page 50, make and label flower centers with numerals. Cut out several flower petals in various colors. Let the children put the correct number of petals on each flower.

✔ Put numerals on several small flowerpots. Provide single stems of artificial flowers. Have the children put the correct number of flowers in each pot. (Place a little Styrofoam or florists' foam in the bottom of each pot to anchor flowers.)

✔ Provide several of each kind of a variety of seeds or artificial flowers. Let the children use them to create patterns.

✔ Mix several different kinds of seeds or flowers. Have the children sort them into like groups.

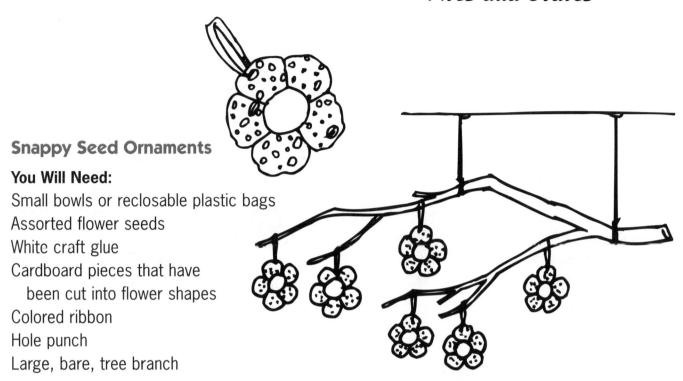

Snappy Seed Ornaments

You Will Need:

Small bowls or reclosable plastic bags

Assorted flower seeds

White craft glue

Cardboard pieces that have
   been cut into flower shapes

Colored ribbon

Hole punch

Large, bare, tree branch

How to Do:

1. Empty the flower seeds into small individual bowls or reclosable plastic bags.
2. Punch a hole in the top of the flower-shaped cardboard.
   Thread the ribbon through the hole and tie a knot to secure.
3. Glue the different kinds of seeds onto the flower-shaped cardboard.
4. Hang the flowers on a large branch in your room.

Popcorn Apple Blossoms

You Will Need:

Light blue construction paper

Brown and green tempera paint or markers

White glue

Popped popcorn

How to Do:

1. With brown paint or marker, draw a large tree branch on the blue paper.
2. Add some green leaves with the paint or marker.
3. To create the apple blossoms, glue the popped popcorn onto the tree branch.

Flower Cart

You Will Need:

Flower stickers

Scissors

9 ½" pipe cleaners

Cardboard

Plastic berry cartons

Small tissue-paper or silk flowers

How to Do:

1. Cut two circle shapes from the cardboard.
   Stick a flower stamp or sticker onto the center
   of each cardboard "wheel." Glue to the sides of the berry carton.
2. Bend a pipe cleaner in half, folding it over to form a handle. Weave it
   into the open spaces of the berry carton. (Be to extend the pipe cleaner
   as far below the cart as the front wheels to help stabilize it.)
3. Fill the berry carton with small tissue-paper or silk flowers.

Painting Flowers with Straws

You Will Need:

Tempera paint, thinned

12" x 18" white watercolor paper

Drinking straws

Paint shirts

How to Do:

1. **Always start at the bottom edge of the
   paper.** Drop a large blob of dark green paint
   near the bottom edge of the paper. Place a
   straw very close to the paint and blow the
   paint up across the paper, making the stem
   and/or branches.
2. Drop blobs of brightly colored paint at the top
   of the stems. Blow with the straw so the paint
   resembles flowers with petals (or whatever
   design the child desires).
3. Add lighter green drops of paint to blow
   for leaves.

Flowering Frame

You Will Need:

Magnet-backed, plain picture frame
  (available in craft stores)
Several colors of silk flowers
Buttons
Bows
White craft glue
Children's photos

How to Do:

1. Glue the flowers, buttons, and bows around the edges of the picture frame. (You may want to ask the mothers to send in little plastic things that would remind them of their child to also glue around the frame. For example: little airplanes or cars, little Barbie shoes, letters of the alphabet, etc.)
2. After the glue has dried, take a Polaroid picture of the child and place it in the frame.

Handprint Birds

You Will Need:

12″ x 18″ construction paper, assorted colors
Several sponges
  (one for each color of paint used)
Several colors of paint, including white
Scissors
Tub filled with water and soap for washing
  hands immediately
Paper towels

How to Do:

1. Press the child's right hand onto a paint-soaked sponge, then press it onto the paper. Repeat this with the left hand. Let the paint dry.
2. After the paint is dry, draw or paint the head, beak, eyes, and the tail of the bird.
 * For very young children, cut out the shapes of the bird's head, beak, eyes, and tail and have them glue the shapes onto their handprints.

Snack Time

Flower Pot Flurry

You Will Need:
4 4" terra-cotta pots
Large bowl
Large spoon
Small spoon
Measuring cup
Cookie sheet

Ingredients:
4 round peanut butter cookies
⅓ cup peanut butter
⅓ cup Karo syrup
1 cup crisp rice cereal
½ cup strawberry jelly
2 pints vanilla ice cream, softened
Peanuts
Prepared strawberry topping

How to Do:
1. Place peanut butter cookies in the bottom of the terra cotta pots.
2. Combine peanut butter, corn syrup, and cereal. Mix well.
3. Spread thinly around the insides of the pots.
4. Spread jelly over the peanut butter mixture. (The jelly will spread more evenly if warmed first.)
5. Spoon ice cream into the pots, fill to the top, and place in the freezer.
6. Before serving, sprinkle with peanuts and drizzle with strawberry topping.

Picking Flowers

You Will Need:
Toothpicks
Colored plastic wrap
Ribbon

Ingredients:
Caramels
Gumdrops

How to Do:
1. Unwrap each caramel and stick five toothpicks into the outer edges.
2. Select five gumdrops and slide them onto the ends of the toothpicks.
3. Wrap the flower in colored plastic wrap and tie together with a ribbon.

Flowering Fruit Pizzas

You Will Need:
Cutting board
Knife

Ingredients:
Banana bread slices or bagels
Strawberry glaze or jelly
Fruits: kiwi, grapes, peaches,
   strawberries, raspberries,
   blueberries

How to Do:
1. Spread bread or
   bagels with a thin layer of the
   strawberry glaze or jelly.
2. Slice the fruits into small pieces.
3. Decorate with the fruits to make flower designs.

Crazy Daisies

You Will Need:
Flower-shaped biscuit cutter
Cutting board
Cookie sheet

Ingredients:
Refrigerated biscuit dough
Sugar/cinnamon mixture

How to Do:
1. Remove biscuits from can and place on the cutting board.
   Cut a flower shape from each biscuit using the flower-
   shaped biscuit cutter. Sprinkle with sugar and cinnamon.
2. Roll extra bits of dough into leaves and a stem. Bake
   according to directions on can. (Be sure to make the extra
   bits of dough rather thick so they will cook evenly with the
   flower part of the biscuit.)

Fantastic Fruit Flowers

You Will Need:
Coffee filter
Small, clean terra cotta pot
Knife
Cutting board
Spoons
Colorful ribbon

Ingredients:
Favorite fruit dip or yogurt
Spinach leaves, optional
Your choice of fruits: apple
   slices, bananas cut in half,
   lengthwise, peaches,
   pears, oranges, grapes

How to Do:
1. Place the coffee filter in the bottom of the terra cotta pot.
2. Spoon the fruit dip or yogurt onto the coffee filter.
3. Arrange the fruits into the dip to resemble a plant, bouquet or flower arrangement. (You can add spinach leaves to resemble the flowers leaves.)
4. Tie a ribbon around the terra cotta pot.

Mother's Day Tea Tray

(Send this idea home so that the child can surprise Mom with help from another adult.)

You Will Need:

Bud vase

Dishes

Silverware

Special card (designed by you or use the borde design below)

Recipe of pink heart French toast bites, coffee or tea, yogurt, Bacon

How to Do:

1. Prepare your mom's favorite recipes. (Another adult will need to help here.)
2. Decorate the tea tray with a fresh flower in the vase and everything else Mom will need for breakfast in bed.
3. Get everything ready before Mom wakes up and deliver to her bedside for a sweet surprise.

Pretty In Pink (Mother's Day Surprise)
Pink Hearts (French toast bites)

You Will Need:
Medium bowl
Whisk
Heart-shaped cookie cutter
Skillet
Plate
Sugar shaker

Ingredients:
2 eggs
½ cup milk
Pinch of cinnamon
Slices of bread, cut into heart shapes
1 tablespoon butter
Pink powered sugar
Fresh raspberries, optional

How to Do:
1. Combine the eggs, milk, and cinnamon in a bowl and whisk until well blended.
2. Dip both sides of each slice of heart-shaped bread in the batter until well soaked. Transfer to a plate.
3. Heat the skillet. Add about ⅓ of the butter. When the butter has melted, add 1 or 2 slices of the soaked bread. Cook over medium heat for about 5 minutes, or until browned. Flip and fry on the other side until light brown.
4. Place heart-shaped French toast on a plate and sprinkle with pink sugar.

Faith Foundations

A mother is a special gift from God. God gave mothers to children to take care of them and love them just as God made them to be. People everywhere share a common bond in honoring their mother. Except for Christmas, Mother's Day is the most popular special day of the year. In your discussions of mothers, make sure to mention the love, help, care, and discipline they give as they model God's love and teach about living as God's children.

To build a faith foundation in the children during this unit, take a look at what God tells us about mothers.

God chose Mary to be the mother of Jesus (Luke 2:6–7). She was a very special lady. Mary took care of Jesus as He grew from a baby to a young man. She loved Jesus and learned from Him.

Scripture

Honor your father and mother (Matthew 19:19a).

Questions

Q What do you like best about your mom?

Q What does it mean to honor your mom?

Q Name some things you could do to help your mom.

Activities

✘ Make a Mother's Scrapbook: Take pictures of the children in your class throughout the school year. Have them each make a special scrapbook that can be laminated and given as a surprise for Mother's Day. (Be sure to include candid shots so Mom will get a feel for life in her child's classroom.) You may use the child's handprint for the cover.

✘ Collect the children's or families' favorite recipes and compile them into a book to share with all of the mothers. Have each child make a food collage from food pictures of their favorite foods, laminate it, and use it as their personal cookbook cover. (If you don't necessarily want to provide working recipes, ask the children to dictate to you how they *think* the dish is prepared.)

✘ Make a group list of all of the ways children could help their mom. Make sure to include things like obey, pick up toys, be kind to brother or sister.